FOOD FOR THE WINTER

FOOD FOR THE WINTER

Poems by
GERALDINE CONNOLLY

PURDUE UNIVERSITY PRESS
West Lafayette, Indiana

Published 1990

Library of Congress Cataloging-in-Publication Data

Connolly, Geraldine, 1947-
  Food for the winter : poems / by Geraldine Connolly.
    p.   cm.
  ISBN 1–55753–005–X (alk. paper) :
  I. Title.
PS3553.05135F6   1990
811'.54--dc20   89-70186

Printed in the United States of America

—*for Steve, and for Sarah and Brian*

CONTENTS

II

III

ACKNOWLEDGMENTS

Acknowledgment is made to the following publications for poems that have appeared or are forthcoming:

Antioch Review: "A Chinese Bowl"; *Arete:* "The World War II Museum, Normandy"; *Denver Quarterly:* "Our Mother Tongue"; *5 A.M.:* "Nail and Hammer"; *The Georgia Review:* "Polish Dolls"; *The Gettysburg Review:* "At Mimi's Style Shop"; *High Plains Literary Review:* "Irwin, Pennsylvania, 1955"; *Nimrod:* "Food for the Winter"; *Pacific Review:* "The August Dark"; *The Pennsylvania Review:* "Summer"; *Poetry:* "Lydia," "The Entropy of Pleasure"; *Poetry Northwest:* "Inside the Blue Train," "In the Family Scene"; *Quarry West:* "From Milkweed Pods"; and *West Branch:* "Elk Horn, Montana," "Ghost Ranch."

Some of these poems have appeared in a chapbook, *The Red Room,* published by Heatherstone Press, Meadville, Pennsylvania.

"Lydia" appeared in *The 1987 Arvon Anthology,* Arvon Foundation, Lancashire, England.

"Letters from France" appeared in *Free State: A Harvest of Maryland Poets,* SCOP Press.

Jean Johnson, Nan Fry, Jeanne Braham, and Victoria Morgan provided invaluable assistance in revising and shaping the manuscript.

The author would also like to thank the National Endowment for the Arts, the Maryland Arts Council, and the Corporation of Yaddo for fellowships that made the completion of this book possible.

I

OUR MOTHER TONGUE

My aunts held it behind their lips,
and would spit out the flames
at each other when they needed
to keep secrets from the children.
And my grandmother had it but kept it
hidden. She was the quiet one,
of great sadness. Language slept
inside her like a sleeping map
of the old country until it was
passed to my mother whose pen
skittered over creamy sheets
like a tall ship carrying messages
over the ocean to those who were left
in the cities of straw and cathedrals.
The trumpet notes travelled
the thin air in blizzards
of sons and daughters forgetting
even their names in the sharp winds
of Pittsburgh and Chicago, the words
melting as they touched
the hard ground of a new land.

THE HEART'S CURTAIN

In his room in the basement, Uncle
rigged up a cunning cat's cradle,
attached it to the Winchester
and pulled the string.
We opened it, saw everything. Who could
forget the avalanche of lilies, the coffin
sailing like a dark boat among them.
Who could forget the whispers about
what happened during the war. When
we push aside the curtain, more curtain
appears, the inside of a rose
opening above its thorny stem
suddenly, on the November altar.
Now we hear the sound of the rifles,
in a seventeen-gun salute,
ringing and ringing.

IN THE FAMILY SCENE

Cold pack, cold cream, dry ice.
I sit at my mother's dressing table
watching the glass eyes of a mink
stare from the rim of a brocade chair.

Among the cut-glass perfume jars,
the Charles of the Ritz lipstick,
vials of fingernail polish lift
their pointed caps like claws.

In the drawer rests the paper hyacinth
I've cut and curled and crayoned
just for her. Beside it, there's a baby
hat crocheted in green that belonged

to my younger sister, my older brother's
ringlets, bright filaments pressed into
a special first-born envelope,
and a bottle of perfume never opened

from the Niagara honeymoon. Dressing up,
she puts on a strapless dress
with tier upon tier of hot pink pleats.
It is for her I bring home *papier-mâché* fish,

watercolors, leaders' capes. For her
I battle my older brother, strong,
dark as an olive and sit
on my charming sister's chest.

My father stands over the bed,
rumpled, smelling of Old Spice
and linseed oil. But where am I?
Under the glass on top of her bureau

in photos with my spelling trophies.
My brother and sister in a beach frame
stand in the next shot holding their sticks
toward me like spears.

DESIGNS WITH FIRE

In the front yard of the brick house
my father built for us after the war,

my mother sat in the grass
with my small, naked sister on her lap.

They lazed under the catalpa shade
as I ran through the irises, past silver fins

on the blue Desoto. Everyone had a lawn
and a brick house. It was 1954.

When the snow came, we rolled
it into balls, constructed an ice fort

where bitter battles occurred.
My brother had a BB gun that he held

in front of the windows of air, scowling
to scare away intruders. When my parents

were gone, he hid in the basement
near the coal bin and started small fires

with scraps of paper, a tiny Vulcan,
his face lit with the power of a struck match.

Stacks of blackened matches mounted
like tiny effigies next to him.

He would make what he wished
appear in the air; invisible writing left

the white scar of what-has-been.
Our uncle had just died, at thirty-five

of a coronary. The red pain seared
through his chest like an ingot

at the mill where he worked. He became
a match consuming itself, lighting

the faces around him
as he shuddered into thin air.

GODMOTHERS

I wanted them to come from God,
but they were orphans Mother said
slowing the word so deliciously

it almost stuck to the roof
of her mouth. We called them "aunt,"
Ann, Eve, Flo—water syllables.

When they played pinochle
with the real aunts and uncles,
they stuck out like garden markers.

The Rendulich sisters, childless,
straightbacked at the oak table;
no fairy tale could have contained them,

bony and gaunt, thumbing
their cards, then touching
a fingertip to their tongues.

Each had her own illness,
complicated and distinct
as their mosaic pillboxes.

Faces flushed with nicotine and rouge,
they picked out colored pills
from silver compartments precisely

on the hour. We loved our evenings
with them, flavored by horehound drops
and whispers of the doctor's critical visit.

Their sweater clips were clipped shut
beneath stern jabots. A crystal
paperweight one of them

stiffly presented me once
held hickory leaves, trapped
and dry inside its glacier.

LYDIA

There was life before us

my sister and I discovered,
looking at photographs

we shouldn't have been looking at
of the English girl my father

was engaged to during the war.
Here she is right in front of our eyes,

the woman before my mother,
in a black lace cocktail dress,

a cigarette in a holder,
pensive, earthy—waiting

in front of the carved wooden radio,
for news from the front.

This is the war, after all,
and here she is again, somewhere

on an English beach, draped
across my father's shoulder

all of her silky skin radiant
above the soft folds of sundress.

They stand in front of a sign
that reads "Seaside Cottages,

two dollars." And here she is
again, painted onto the cockpit

of my father's plane with hardly
anything on at all, and here he is

in his flight jacket, looking,
in fact, happy. My sister and I each

lift our pencils like cigarettes,
taking long sultry drags to puff

out invisible rings. They rise
in the air like silver nooses

that will catch our father
and hold him to us.

THE WORLD WAR II MUSEUM, NORMANDY

The country near the sea lies in fog,
with rows of white grave markers,
chains of pearls stretching to the sea.
In the museum, a mannequin of Josef Mengele
is so devastatingly handsome and evil
we are stunned, and a large steel bomb
remains, like the ones you dropped,
forty times over Europe, Father.

Gray B-25 bombers and army tanks rust,
next to the wavy-haired young man
caught smiling into the camera lens,
left leg lifted jauntily onto the running board
of a '41 Ford. I can only imagine
him, crawling fearfully from a bunk
in the dark, slipping on his leather jacket

and climbing into the cockpit that rumbled
into the black sky. How he did his job,
guiding the pilot through red days,
through smoke and flak as he plotted the flight charts,
measured the distances, rechecked them,

then returned to barracks to sleep
and dream of shiny cars next to foundries
and the heat of trains, willows bending
above creeks. And then to begin his life.

FOOD FOR THE WINTER

My father has no sons
and takes me with him everywhere.
Irwin, Pennsylvania, 1955, and I am seven,
pleased to go to Butler's Hardware
for threepenny nails, to Standard Auto
for motor oil. I tag along
to the slaughterhouse where
we buy food for the winter.

Like a son, I do not hold
his hand. My father says
to the man covered by a white apron.
"We need a side of beef for the winter."
I lean into the glass and look
at the white and red world
everything frigid and clean
as I imagine the Antarctic.
A strange, sweet odor pervades.
Everywhere, the men have huge hands.

Soon bored, I wander off.
Men in white tramp around
slamming freezers shut. Behind
the huge steel door, I catch
a glimpse of a large carcass
hanging from a ceiling hook
my red Christmas coat from
my closet hanger. When no one
is looking, I wander over to a hole
drilled into the wall at the end of the room.

It is a gray room with no windows.
Three men drag a reluctant cow
into the center. She bellows,
an unearthly, piercing bawl.
I hold onto the wall
and look for my father.
He is far away, on the other side
of the room, across the world,
chatting pounds and prices
with the butcher.

I can't help looking
through the hole. The cow,
down on her knees, screams.
I can smell her hair,
see her warm nostrils quiver and curl.
She digs in her hooves.
She slips as they pull her across
the floor. The rope cuts her neck.
They tighten it some more.

I want to cover the hole
but, cold and white,
the cow's bellow travels.
With the sudden crack of the pistol,
the dark stain spreads across her forehead.
Eyes closed, she falls
and the men begin their silent work.

The organs, like strange dark fruits
are shovelled up and removed.
Soon, all that remains are two red mountains
with white veins winding through them like roads.
The hairs on the butcher's wrist are blond
and soft as a baby's. The men hose down
the floor to white and gleaming.

My father, calling from far away,
is waving, business finished.
When we walk out into the light
of the autumn afternoon, I hear
my shoes clatter in the stillness.
I do not take his hand.

IRWIN, PENNSYLVANIA, 1955

Here, on the left, my hometown.
Main Street's slow and not very wide.
You can get about anything at Charlie's store
on the corner; lipstick, tobacco, Hershey kisses.
The old men outside tugging on their suspenders
then spitting into the gutter
are mannequins, fixed and forever.
I am eight years old, waiting for Mr. Mancini
to patch and shine my Sunday patent leathers.

The Infant of Prague sits, ruffled and crimped
on his stand in the corner. Cops patrol
the alley after five, and through the glass
of the pizza parlor windows, I watch the hoods
in dark jackets looking for trouble. They
slick back their oily curls and stick combs
under rolled sleeves. They practice their
wolf whistles from the hoods of revved-up Chevies;
I pay no mind.

Academy girls don't wear shorts or look for trouble.
When they hoot and catcall, I drift by,
admire the gowns in the Bon Ton window.
I walk to the library, a large white house
at the end of Main Street. Its porch opens
like a mother's arms. When I go upstairs,
the librarian's sobbing, ready to confide
in a child. Her husband's gone for good this time.
I climb into a book and spread my wings.

NEW TERRITORY

Sent off to boarding school
at twelve, with a pair of oxfords,
a pair of patents, my sterling
silver christening rosary
and two dozen name tags stitched
like drops of blood into the collars
of starched blouses, I stare
down the hall, long and dim,
slippery from too many waxings.
Plaster statues of the holy family live
here, in cave-like niches, the Blessed Virgin,
her face soft and chalky, cheeks
powdered pink. Everything about her
is pliable; she is to be our model.
Joseph is nondescript, covered by
a long brown robe. The baby sleeps.
I eye the nuns, black and fluttery,
and my parents, in wool, with fur collars,
giddy with their new freedom.
I unpack my suitcase and survey
the territory. One iron bed,
one chest of drawers, one slender closet.
A crucifix pierces the white wall.
A dark trunk opens its jaws
to swallow my life.

LETTERS FROM FRANCE

Locked up with the nuns day and night,
we took French, wrote passionate plays,
went to Mass, Benediction, Vespers,
and the Stations of the Cross
and sometimes sneaked to the park
to light up a Tareyton and pretend
we knew what screwing was about.
Soeur Celine suggested we take
up pen pals from France.

When that first letter arrived,
in the thin, elegant, rippled envelope,
we shook as we walked up to Sister Charlotte's desk,
importantly, to receive our mail from Paris.
We ripped it open as though the ancient secrets
of the Gauls were revealed inside. We could never get
enough mail from Jean-Pierre with words
like *chemise,* or *pommes de terre.*
Soon, dark pictures taken in train stations,
tittery jokes and invitations for visits
flew back and forth across the ocean.

We knew nothing yet of the thunder
about to seize our bodies.
So we wrote and wrote. And we waited
for the letter back with its dark, inky,
jagged handwriting rising on the page
like the crest of some huge wave
about ready to break over us,
across our single beds and crucifix,
our pleated skirts hanging
in the closet above our saddle shoes.

EASTER VIGIL

All day we tarry
at Christ's tomb,
the chapel steeped
in purple sorrow,
candles unlit,
our bodies lean
from fasting.

For three days,
the Lord is not with us.
We remember his journey
and pray for the dead
their names muffled
gunshots among us.
The novices file into chapel
in white veils, black drapery,
all his young brides, quiet,
so as not to wake him.

He sleeps in white linen.
We wait for him
like the buried flowers
who press upward
against the earth.

OUR PARENTS ARE GONE FOR THE DAY

All the wheat is glaring in the fields
and cousin Sandra won't let us have oatmeal.
She lounges on the swing, dressed in curlers
and chenille, catching us with the tip
of a fly swatter when we step too close.
In the morning, she orders us to snap beans
and shuck corn. Before lunch,
we scrub the bathroom floors. To get
our supper, Sandra commands "Sing like clowns."
Her younger sister, who refuses, feels
the smart of a belt on her back. Sandra
threatens us all with death if we tell. Before
the adults get back, we all sit down to
Monopoly, scrubbed and pajamaed, sweet
as Giotto's cherubs. Sandra's hair is silk and her skin
is cream. She is the May Queen that year,
wearing an eyelet gown, lifting lilies to
the virgin's arms in the glossy photo
she sends at Christmas. To think, says my mother,
sighing with envy at her sister's good luck,
your blood cousin.

FROM MILKWEED PODS

From out of the cloud of seeds,
they fly towards us, arms and legs flapping,
towheaded cousins. Blue eyes, hazel eyes,
pigtails, crewcuts, everywhere cousins.
At christenings, at funerals, cousins
in the front parlor, at the piano
or dancing with the bride, wolfing down
pancakes, veils awry at Communion breakfasts.
With babies on their laps, waving cotton candy
torches or slingshots, they scream down
roller coasters at some wild amusement park.
Cousins in the attic, cousins under the bed
with lumps of coal in their Christmas stockings.
Cousins, solemn and angelic, singing hymns
at Vegelia dinner. We are playing
Monopoly, Scrabble, Blind Man's Bluff. We are
running through the fields together searching
for the lost cow, searching for the one-eyed horse.
Grandmother is alive and scolding us in Polish,
cousins about to leap from the hayloft, bats
skimming their hair, a stream of cousins
in a line like a moving rope calling
through the thin spring air, "Red Rover,
we dare you. Come over."

AT MIMI'S STYLE SHOP

The appointment is my first.
A whole hour is mine. Each square
of hair parts under Mimi's comb
each wisp pinched into a silver clip.
Robed figures float across the mirrors.
When the cutting begins, I go dull.

So she takes my hair. The shades close.
I am a lamb in her hands. The shears
love me. Then she tugs my hair
into ropes and rolls it tight.
If beauty hurts like this, then
how must love feel. In the women's
magazines, I see dangerous examples.
The rollers dig. She sticks some picks in.
Under the silver dome of dryer, I burn.
She turns up the heat and leaves.

When my hair is dry—bone dry and stiff,
she tears out the curlers and teases
it up into a bubbled hive. Then I am handed
a mirror to admire each side as the boys
at the dance will admire. And I am unpinned,
the kimono hung on a nail. I am misted
with a spray of Aqua Net to hold the curves.
My father comes in the blue car.
I am sent out, coiffed, curled,
and limp as a cutout doll. Locks
of my hair are gone and I am dizzy with style.
Tonight the boys will take my hand,
smile as my father does now,
call out my name.

II

POLISH DOLLS

The first doll, fat and round,
an autumn pear with cheeks on fire,
smiles, benign, and pats her belly.
She is the first aunt, the oldest, Blanche.
Her hair is parted in the middle, neatly.
She carries a basket of eggs and parsley
and one is surprised to find she comes apart.
Inside of her is a plump sister, Helen,
a parenthesis smaller, still egg-shaped
with an identical nose. She is always waving
a yellow spoon and her shoes are crude and heavy.
A trowel in her hand continually
digs up some new earth although
she never moves out of her backyard.
And inside of her is a thinner sister
the mouth large and sensuous as a dahlia.
The hands look outstretched.
There was a violin between them once.
Now they are empty. Inside this doll
is yet another sister, Sally,
her head cowled. Finally,
the eyebrows have become bold
but the structure of her backbone
is not quite strong enough. Her mouth,
pinched like a penny, grins.
She, too, breaks in half

and inside is the slenderest twig
of a sister. There is no kerchief
on her head, only a small curl of yarn.
The eyebrows are gone. She is about
to pick up a missal and pray.
The smallest dab of a red nose
has been brushed on and the eyes
are almost not there. The expression
on her watercolor face is hard to read.
It is either acceptance or terror.
And within the last doll
is the smallest sister. I look closely
and see that she is my mother,
hands only thin brushstrokes of rose,
as though they are not really meant.
She is the infant we don't expect
to last the winter. The others stare
like useless clerics at this fatherless doll.
There is no seam that opens her up.
The stripes on her dress circle like o's
a pebble makes when hitting the water.

PORCELAIN

The dingy buildings
stand behind her sullen
dark cloud of hair. I think

of the room
where she gave birth
to her firstborn,

my brother, with no doctor.
The child came hard and fast,
the way love had come to her.

She was not ready to be a mother.
There are many things she won't
let herself remember,

her father taken early,
her brothers sent to work
in the glass factory.

Even after her new husband,
even after my birth,
she still couldn't be happy.

We see it in the pictures.
He would scream when she left
the room for a moment.

There was no peace. So we tried
to be peaceful for her, my sister
and I, to make up for her father's death

for my brother's fury,
her first husband's cruelty.
My sister and I were our mother's

mothers, passing our hands
over her face like soft towels,
exalted by her sadness.

THE WOMEN WHO
CALLED MY FATHER AT NIGHT

for solace, for kindness
from the labor union president
poured out their spinsterish hearts
to him like wine from a never ending bottle,
Lucy, with her harelip and collection of china dolls,
stuttering out his name as we answered,
Sylvia, with her platinum blonde hair
and pencilled eyebrows, purring over her problems,
Shirley, with one medical emergency after another:
slipped discs, sties, eczema.
How we all wondered what they were saying
as we eavesdropped from our cozy kitchen table,
reading or playing cards. I listened to him
console these lonely women, gently.
They must have hated to hang up
their phones and return
to single beds and tables set
for one. They must have hated to sever
the connection to his deep, soothing
voice, rumbling over the line.

SUMMER

The irises came on strong
and the corn didn't come up till August.
We would swing and rock on the front porch
watching lightning bugs leap through the night.
That was the summer the cows got into
the alfalfa field and blew up like balloons.
That was the summer Blanche died.
Jack brought a girl home only
two months after the funeral and slept
with her in Blanche's cherry high poster.
Bats got in the barn and we couldn't
get them out. That was the summer Jack
and the hired man got drunk and drove
the tractor in circles through the low field
and ended up in the stream. The mockingbirds
sang late into the night. That was the summer
Jack fell asleep in bed with a lit cigarette
and burned the house down. He slept like a baby.
Never woke up. The china burnt up,
Blanche's crochet work, the family pictures,
the clock on the mantel from New York.
They could see Jack's fire from ten miles around.

THE LINENS OF
THE SISTERS OF ST. VINCENT

The nuns at Benediction,
we are in the forbidden hall
rifling through their lingerie,
shrieking, tying their cotton slips
around our heads like turbans,
dancing in Mother Ildefonse's bloomers.

It is even better than looking at natives
in the old issues of *National Geographic*.
We are two tipsy corks in deep water
next to the honeycomb of cubicles
that hold these secret garments.

Giddy with rebellion, we release one after another
flapping into the clean winter air.
We send the brassiere of our fat cook, Sister Philomena,
out next to Father Ryan's underwear. We slingshot
Sister Charlotte's panties all the way

to the furthest limb of the high evergreen.
Exultant, we send one last garment out
and it flies, landing lonely, glowing
with the sad light of a beached trout.
And then we head up to our rooms
with the news that they, like us,
have skin under their robes,
flesh aside from their holy faces
and swim the insistent tides of the body.

SUNDAY

Sunday mass, the hard blond pews
yellow as saint's bones that I knew
were hidden in the altar stone.
Snow melts on shawls all along

the row in front of us. My sister
and I genuflect and cross
ourselves, fingers flecked
with cold holy water.

Our mother dropped us
here among satin chasubles
rippling along the altar,
pious heads nodding amidst incense

and the terror of bells,
the low mumbling in Latin.
We break into rhythmic standing,
sitting, kneeling and inhale

the perfume of lilies lifting
from necks. We intone
the names of the departed:
they are stones in our mouths.

Now the priest asks us
to give up whatever we love
the most, candy or anger,
for God who wants more

than we think we can give.
He wants abstinence.
Like a train shuddering
through slums, he moves

through our sins and then
mixes wine with the water.
We eat the dry bread,
dissolving it on our tongues.

THE LETTERS OF HIS NAME

We couldn't take our eyes off
her zigzag of scabs, the lightning
shape of her wound that flashed red
when she lifted her hand. She loved him
enough to draw blood from her own wrist

piercing it with needles.
Row after row of pinpricks
must have flowed into each other,
streams of red engraved in her cells
that dried into the letters of his name.

We younger cousins stared, awestruck,
above our ruffled socks, tight shoes.
Along the pale canvas of her skin,
these red spiky flowers flared, exotic
next to the blue solemn tributaries
of veins that she had reached
close to, snaring proofs of her love.

I wondered about their future.
For now, they could be hidden
under a sleeve as her passion had been
but when the cuts healed, a scar
would remain, the white puffy letters
chaotic forever on her smooth skin.

She slammed her door on us
but we remained, entranced,
outside her room listening
for the painful syllables that escaped
from whirling disks on her turntable,
silver needle tongue in groove.

THE AUGUST DARK

The summer I was fifteen,
floating on a raft in Canada,
drowsy in my pink bathing suit,
I met the first boy I loved.
Later that evening, he roared
up in his speedboat to the dock
of our summer house. Nervous, awestruck
by this boy in chinos with a hard walk,
white sweater slung across his shoulders,
I slid, in the warm dusk,
into the radiant interior
of his boat. A fishing lure
caught on my sock. Glittery,
double-pronged, with a red eye,
its silver body flashed
as we banged across the waves
to the Ojibway Lodge, where,
at a cabin in the pine woods,
we watched a handsome count
romance Sophia Loren. We held hands
and burned in the dark. I can remember
the sunset's vivid flare as we walked
wordless, back to the boat.
The moon a pale hook, we rode
with his arm around my waist,
fast across the waves,
the warm night opening before us.
I still think of the dark
as a lover, covering
my shoulders like a boy's coat.
I was so reckless, so shy I could
hardly look up into his eyes
while, on my sock, like a promise
the silver lure glittered, stuck.

THE ENTROPY OF PLEASURE

By the time you walk up to the ocean
the wave has already disappeared, another sadness
as in passion, or the light dying at dusk

or the shell split under your foot, another
scar made in the sand. You can't remember
exactly what you need to remember. White fluttering

wings arrive in the sweet grass like letters
from someone you loved who has abandoned you
for another city. And all the signs

read "Dangerous Currents," "Sea Forest"
and lead to unexpected climates. Change is a way
we can't easily follow, the water disappearing.

Even the dunes have shifted and right
when you are about to lose your way
into the wild oats, shuddering,

there are the stars in the center
of sand dollars that make you remember
what you spent is spent, the entropy

of pleasure a wave's body you can't hold
in your hands. You know the only way
out is landmarks you can't imagine.

the way we are drawn, pulled by the tides,
a first step into happiness, its dangerous currents
licked by the water's green flames.

NAIL AND HAMMER

I am thinking of the comet that sails
through the universe, unbearably light, pulled
by a black chariot, howling wolves.
Tonight white streets are filled
with sleepwalkers piercing the fog
like needles, and trees, swaying,
holding their burden of leaves bravely
in the green dark and white souls
flying up from their graves to hurl
themselves against cold windows.
I am thinking of pigeons climbing fire escapes
or lifting off from slumbering boats.
I am thinking of the fierceness of sex,
how we hammer furiously against each other
in the dark, how we wake hungry for each other.
I am thinking of how the sun rises, day after day,
holding its juicy flesh towards us to eat,
of how we come upon the hard pit of night.

III

A CHINESE BOWL

I'm awake.
All the lights of the house
glitter in honor of your return.
I've painted this room the color
of a plum and set out
blue candles and a Chinese bowl.
On its side is a country scene
of crested mountains and three trees
above a lake. All the neighborhood
sleeps.

In the night sky above us
you are winging home in a silver plane
from the other side of the world.
You are above the Pacific now
above the Sierras. You cross
the wheat fields of Kansas,
a thousand lakes. And now, love,
you sleep, sprawled across two seats,
dreaming of hibiscus
and the stars hurtle you through
the blue space between us.

An old man on the bowl stands
fishing high above the lake.
The line trembles fiercely
as he brings his catch to earth.

INSIDE THE BLUE TRAIN

Among the curtains frosted with light,
through panels of white roses,
we see the sky outside,
turning like a Ferris wheel.

We pull up our chairs
to the table, smooth our napkins
against our laps and raise goblets
to make a toast, clinking and clinking
like the thousand prisms of chandeliers

that shiver above us. The light even
now is letting go of its flame,
emptying its palm and passing
upwards to enter the prisms of glass
as guests enter the dining room and seat

themselves, politely pull up their chairs
and flicker like stars in a planetarium
against the rows of primrose
and thistle gathering on the walls.
A caravan of waiters proceeds

carrying platters of food,
timbales like snowy mountains,
moons floating in oyster shells,
crescents of tangerine in golden rows.
Everywhere the spoons lift and sparkle,

enter the river of mouths like boats
among the soft murmurs of ice and water,
of rolls and butter lifted and spread,
of salt falling softly on meat. Swans drift
among the saltcellars, orchis and yellow violet
rising from their wings in sprays.

The air is filled with the music
of spoons, the luxurious light
of October or golden bells.
We are inside a train that travels
across the voices singing in churches
their domes rising like peaches.

Even the cattle, when we try
to find them in the dark window,
step forth gently from the clouds
like stars that every moment move
whiter and closer. We feel
their warm breaths in the dark,
open our palms and offer
bread we have saved for them.

DRAGONFLY, LILY, WHITE SKULL

Here I lie, naked, flat on my back
on the cold white table.
Heels in stirrups, my knees scissor
and fold above the doctor's head,
bent like a lover's into my hair.
I am a butterfly, about to be pinned
to a board on a silver needle.
Stained glass insects flutter in the air.
Bumblebees and dragonflies swim
from the thin wires of a mobile,
some crazy attempt at distraction.

On the wall beside me, a red and white
map of the female genitalia.
Here I can trace the mystery of my sex,
vulva, ovary, uterus. The river
of fallopia winds its way through this
strange white lily, this bleached skull.
Like bones filled with a sky of hurricanes,
my body once held a daughter, a son,
and delivered them into the ruined garden.

THE RED ROOM

The legs of my daughter rise in a wishbone
above arrows woven into the carpet,
firs and blossom, ladders from nowhere.
Now she draws the bow of her violin
across strings and the notes escape.
Halfway between mantel and window
she stands, adjusting the music stand
to her new height. Here, like an absence
her presence, slender, tenuous. Once
I lay on a bed in a room and heard the wind
bring cold down from the north as it must
have brought me to my mother.

I, too, sat and practiced at scales, white
then black while she lent a distracted ear,
pierced linen with stitches. Finally,
the last note travelling its own distance
as to a city in snow, the blue case shut
and locked, the feet moving
through the hall and the door unfastened.
I see my daughter's absence, a light
left on during the day or the memory
of wind entering my bones like some old sadness
burning impossibly in the bright room.

VICTORY

My son lifts his imaginary bazooka
and points it at the enemy
who are swarming the steps
of the Lincoln Monument. Then he tosses
a few grenades and shrieks
as they strike car after car.
We are on our way to the Museum of History
for the second grade class trip.
His lips twist as bullets
escape his throat. He pushes
the trigger, vibrating as he shoots
the drivers of buses, of trolleys, of vans,
then the policeman on the horse
riding through the green park, all
the government secretaries on park benches,
brown bags blooming from their laps.
The muscular joggers pass in a daze,
their eyes fixed on the distant Potomac,
which lies calm and blue
as water fixed on a map,
as he guns down the circle of tourists
gathered around the monument,
then his teacher, the first grade teacher,
his friends sitting next to him,
and triumphant from his high seat,
watches the shaken leaves of the stunned oak
fall and fall, all of it his gold sphere.

THE THEATER OF CHILDHOOD

My children love to disappear
into the cellar, shutting the white door

to the kitchen behind them. I hear
their footsteps drumroll

on the wooden steps. Their whispering
voices float up through the joists

and turn to high shrill laughter.
They are down there practicing.

I imagine the chenille bedspread
they use as a curtain rising

and falling on their dramas. They play
"Office" and "Library" and "Dance Club."

They spread themselves into life
the way oil spreads across water, shining.

I hear "Pardon me, dear"
and loud shouting. I hear swords

knocking together, the voices
of babies and crones, the howl

of wolves: they are constructing
a village whose roof slates occasionally

clatter to the floor. Draped in shawls,
they steal strawberries from the garden

of the old woman behind the turret
of furnace, who, busy with shovel and fire,

does not see them for now,
and therefore does not break the spell.

HUNTING LODGE

This is a dull Chekhov play
all brocade and Biedermeier
the snow falling inside
glass balls on a Christmas fir.

We have come to this
hunting lodge with the count
and countess, she resplendent
in white satin and cameos

he in his monocle and neat beard,
dancing shoes gleaming
from beneath his striped trousers.
The time is midnight.

A cricket sings on the hearth.
Windows are filling with darkness
and tired children begin to climb
up to their beds in the attic

and peer out at the winter lawn
brightened by an icy sky. Now
they are twining themselves
among sisters and brothers.

Under the heavy blankets, they listen
for owls and mice, the scampering
of feet across rafters. Downstairs,
the madeleines are being passed.

Chamber music ignites. Conversation
enters and leaves the white spaces
like the moon leaving the meadow
while the sleeper is walking.

We all suddenly know what we want,
only this, the cool mountain
of dessert, the floating stories of the guests,
firelight come to power.

O'KEEFFE: FIRST WINTER AT ABIQUIU

Icy lilies.
Into their white flesh
a blue road nearly disappears

like the body I loved.
I have forgotten
the curve of his jawline,

the shade of his skin in afternoon
shadow. The cliffs beyond Abiquiu
have become cold with snow

as they hold him no longer
and now carry the blue road,
a ribbon of disappearance.

Only horses graze here
silent among cottonwoods.
Cactus wear a lace

of snow as if a wedding
or a death has occurred.
I line up a row of shells,

small wonders filled with irises,
lightning, a crack of thunder.
My housekeeper is deaf.

I see her dark form—a large black wing
blocking the light from the door
then, the sky disappears.

Words, harsh and false, will not
be spoken. Only the earth
is true. Its colors speak

to me, carnelian—basalt,
flames burning inside flames,
ceasing to be themselves.

ELK HORN, MONTANA

No elk here, only a brown wreck
of ghost town afloat, windless
in a sea of Douglas fir, ripped
tarpaper atop doorless shacks
and, on one roof, five bleached cow skulls
glistening in the hot light.

On the hill where a small breeze
begins, butterflies roam the house
of the dead, lighting on stones
etched with granite lambs, twisted
caps of angel hair, streaming

fitfully between the wooden markers
of the unnamed. There is a child's grave
marked "Wyman Bell, alive fifteen days,"
and his two sisters, Beatrice and Clara,
who sleep in their beds of clay.

Powdered sugar roses climb
a split fence where a cricket
the color of lead stops.
So here, out of the wind, the stones
look up, as if to remember.

GHOST RANCH

First the row of skulls
and pelvis bones on cedar.

Red dust blew behind us.
A small bell rang in the breeze.

There was a whiteness everywhere
even in the sonata emerging

from a crescent of mountain, like an idea.
We tried it on, forgot about destruction.

Grapes in a dish, purple mountains.
The door to the patio is open.

Sagebrush flares in silver flames.
Beauty in three red stones

a bone on a windowsill,
the light through our fingers.

Geraldine Connolly was born in Greensburg, Pennsylvania. She received her B.A. from the University of Pittsburgh and a master's degree in English from the University of Maryland. She worked on the staff of the Folger Shakespeare Library from 1971 to 1975.

She has received fellowships in poetry from the National Endowment for the Arts and the Corporation of Yaddo. In 1987, she received the Johns Hopkins summer writing conference poetry prize. In 1988, she received a works-in-progress grant from the Maryland Arts Council and was the William Sloane Scholar in poetry at the Breadloaf Writers' Conference.

Her chapbook, *A Red Room,* was published recently by Heatherstone Press. Her work has appeared in *Antioch Review, Poetry, The Georgia Review,* and *Poetry Northwest.* She lives in Bethesda, Maryland, with her husband and two children and teaches at the Writers Center and in the Maryland Poetry-in-the-Schools Program.

MORE POETRY FROM PURDUE

LA PLATA CANTATA
Jim Barnes

"It is a deep new pleasure to come on a poet with the imaginative boldness of Jim Barnes. In addition to his skill, and what might be called a kind of forthright mysticism, Barnes has an almost uncanny ability to pick not only workable subjects for poems but subjects that, but for him, would not have been subjects at all; no one else would have seen them."—James Dickey
76 pages, ISBN 0–911198–96–2, $6.75

FISHING WITH BLOOD
Fleda Brown Jackson

"A splendid collection of poems with the special merit of being both intensely artful and equally interesting. No one to my knowledge has written better about Georgia O'Keeffe, and many have tried. Fleda Brown Jackson has a good wit, a sharp eye, and a tough character."—Dave Smith
96 pages, ISBN 0–911198–94–6, $6.50

THE SPINE
Michael Spence

". . . . a strong, clear collection. Its spare imagery is absolutely appropriate for the human and natural landscapes it evokes with both economy and grace."—Joseph Bruchac
76 pages, illustrated, ISBN 0–911198–89–X, $5.75

A SEASON OF LOSS
Jim Barnes

"[He] moves with assurance from the past to the present, linking them firmly in his vision and helping his readers be authentic in thought and feeling."—William Stafford
80 pages, illustrated, ISBN 0–911198–75–X, $5.50

THE ARTIST AND THE CROW
Dan Stryk

"A reader finds landscapes or settings, and their inhabitants, that come alive in richly textured but unvaryingly precise language."
—Ralph J. Mills, Jr.
96 pages, illustrated, ISBN 0–911198–71–7, $5.25

ALL THAT, SO SIMPLE
Neil Myers

"[He] writes with such artistry that whatever he presents us with appears in its essence."—Arturo Vivante
72 pages, illustrated, ISBN 0–911198–56–3, $4.00